WHAT DOES A POINT GUARD DO?

Paul Challen

PowerKiDS press™

New York

Published in 2017 by The Rosen Publishing Group, Inc.
29 East 21st Street, New York, NY 10010

Developed and Produced for Rosen by BlueApple*Works* Inc.
Managing Editor for BlueApple*Works*: Melissa McClellan
Art Director: Tibor Choleva
Designer: Joshua Avramson
Photo Research: Jane Reid
Editor: Kelly Spence

Basketball is a fluid game; care was taken and every effort was made to portray players in
the identified positions to highlight the content being featured.

Photo Credits: Title page, page borders michelaubryphoto/Shutterstock; title page, p. 8, 12, 16, 20, 22 Aspenphoto/Dreamstime.com;
page backgrounds Eugene Sergeev/Shutterstock; TOC Aleksandar Grozdanovski/Shutterstock; p. 4 T.J. Choleva /EKS/Shutterstock;
p. 5, 10, 14, 17 left, 17 middle, 18, 29 Louis Horch/Dreamstime.com; p. 6, 11, 15, 19 left Aspen Photo/Shutterstock.com; p. 7, 27 right
Keith Allison/Creative Commons; p. 9, 21 Douglas Sacha/Dreamstime.com; p. 13 Michael Turner/Dreamstime.com; p. 15 top, 27
top Jerry Coli/Dreamstime.com; p. 17 right Martin/Dreamstime.com; p. 19 right, 27 left Photo Works/Shutterstock.com; p. 23 Pavel
Shchegolev/Shutterstock.com; p. 24, 28 Monkey Business Images/Shutterstock; p. 25 SpeedKingz/Shutterstock; p. 26 left Erik Drost/
Creative Commons; p. 26 right Verse Photography/Creative Commons

Cataloging-in-Publication Data
Names: Challen, Paul.
Title: What does a point guard do? / Paul Challen.
Description: New York : PowerKids Press, 2017. | Series: Basketball smarts | Includes index.
Identifiers: ISBN 9781508150503 (pbk.) | ISBN 9781508150459 (library bound) |
    ISBN 9781508150336 (6 pack)
Subjects: LCSH: Basketball--Juvenile literature.
Classification: LCC GV885.1 C53 2017 | DDC 796.323--dc23

Manufactured in the United States of America
CPSIA Compliance Information: Batch #BS16PK For Further Information contact: Rosen Publishing, New York, New York at 1-800-237-9932

CONTENTS

THE BASKETBALL TEAM

Basketball is an exciting, fast-paced sport that is fun to both watch and play. During a game, each team has five players on the court, playing in different positions. The five positions include point guard, shooting guard, small forward, power forward, and center. While each position has a different set of responsibilities on the court, to be successful as a team, all five players have to work together.

Each position is assigned a number. This diagram shows where each player is typically positioned when the team is trying to score.

1. **Point guard:** The player who is responsible for leading the team and creating scoring opportunities.

2. **Shooting guard:** A player who focuses on scoring baskets, often from a **wing**, or side, position.

3. **Small forward:** A speedy, skilled player who can score baskets.

4. **Power forward:** A player who uses his or her size to play close to the basket to **rebound** and defend.

5. **Center:** Usually the tallest player on the team, the center plays near the net and shoots, rebounds, and blocks shots.

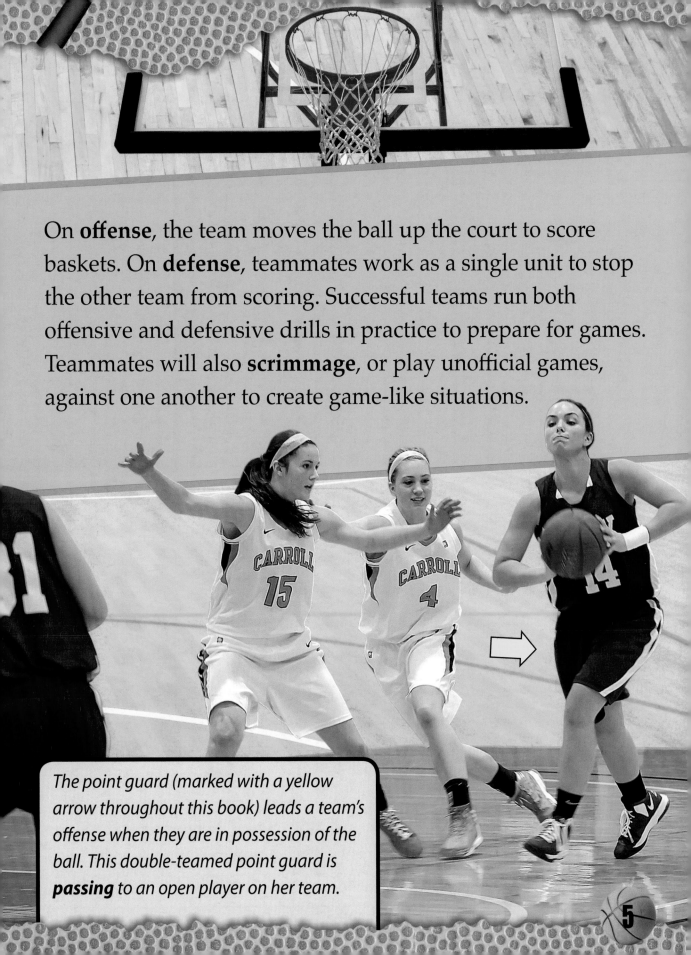

On **offense**, the team moves the ball up the court to score baskets. On **defense**, teammates work as a single unit to stop the other team from scoring. Successful teams run both offensive and defensive drills in practice to prepare for games. Teammates will also **scrimmage**, or play unofficial games, against one another to create game-like situations.

*The point guard (marked with a yellow arrow throughout this book) leads a team's offense when they are in possession of the ball. This double-teamed point guard is **passing** to an open player on her team.*

The point guard on a basketball team is the player often called the leader of the offense. Point guards have the important job of leading their basketball team, just as a general leads an army. Most plays, whether on offense or defense, start with the point guard, who works closely with the coach.

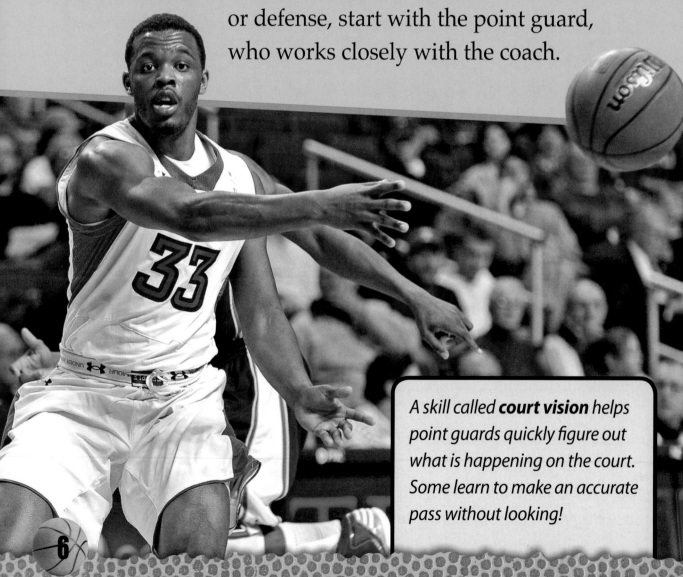

*A skill called **court vision** helps point guards quickly figure out what is happening on the court. Some learn to make an accurate pass without looking!*

In order to run plays, point guards need great ball-handling and passing skills. They must be able to keep control of the ball under pressure from the defense, and get the ball where it needs to go. Although point guards often make the most **assists** for their team in a game, they also must be able to score on their own. The best point guards can do it all: call plays, pass, defend, and score.

Derrick Rose of the Chicago Bulls (right) is about average height for an NBA point guard at 6 feet 3 inches (1.91 m) tall. Often point guards are the shortest and lightest players on their team. Their size makes them fast and agile, which helps them control the ball when they **dribble** and quickly set up plays all over the court.

OFFENSIVE STRATEGY

On offense, point guards often control the pace of the game as they bring the ball up the court. They dictate whether the action on the court is fast or slow. One of the point guard's main jobs is to set up scoring opportunities. From the top of the **key**, he or she looks for weaknesses in the other team's defense and sets up plays to create open players. If a play doesn't work and a teammate gets stuck, the point guard can call for the ball and reset the offense.

A good point guard is always communicating with his teammates. He calls out plays and sets the pace of each attack, taking advantage of a breakaway or slowing the speed if his teammates need to catch their breath. He also keeps an eye on the clock and the scoreboard.

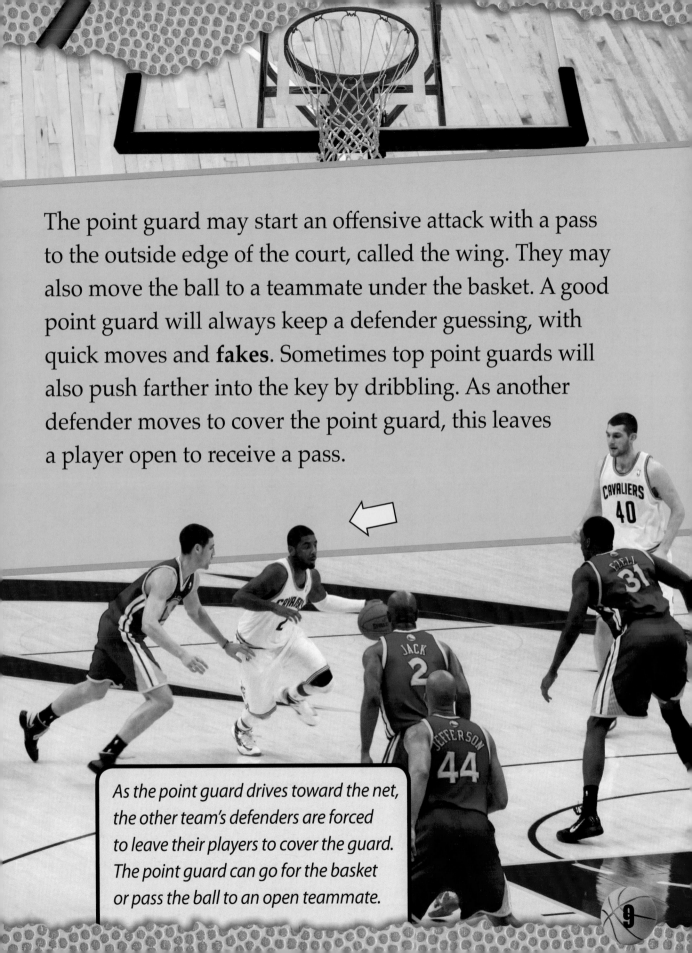

The point guard may start an offensive attack with a pass to the outside edge of the court, called the wing. They may also move the ball to a teammate under the basket. A good point guard will always keep a defender guessing, with quick moves and **fakes**. Sometimes top point guards will also push farther into the key by dribbling. As another defender moves to cover the point guard, this leaves a player open to receive a pass.

As the point guard drives toward the net, the other team's defenders are forced to leave their players to cover the guard. The point guard can go for the basket or pass the ball to an open teammate.

DEFENSIVE STRATEGY

The point guard must also be a good defender. He or she must be able to stop the opponent's best ball handler and break up passing plays. Between sprinting up and down the court, diving after loose balls, and generally being a nuisance on defense, it takes a lot of energy to play point guard.

If a loose ball comes flying down the court, the point guard is usually the player who chases it down to regain possession. It's the point guard's job to try to keep the action in the other team's side of the court.

To play good, active defense, point guards stay in a low, crouching position. They shuffle rapidly from side to side to stay in front of the players they are guarding. It is very important to keep their hands moving as well, to keep pressure on their opponents. When a defender gains possession of the ball by interrupting a dribble or a pass, it is called a **steal**. A point guard has to be careful not to **foul** an opponent while trying to take the ball.

An effective point guard keeps his eyes focused on an opponent's chest or waist to figure out which way the player is going.

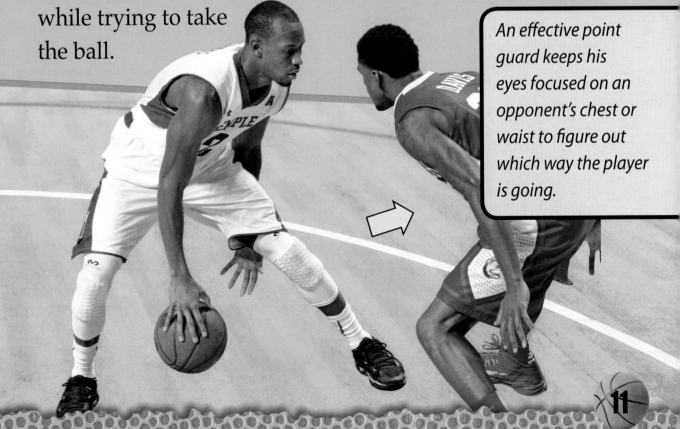

11

BALL HANDLING

One of the most important offensive skills a point guard needs to have is the ability to dribble the ball. To dribble, a player controls the ball by bouncing it up and down using one hand at a time. Point guards need to dribble at all speeds—while running fast or slow, or sometimes even standing still. They also need to have good ball control so their opponents cannot steal the ball.

Point guards are usually the best ball handlers on their team. They bring the ball up the court and keep it moving with turns, pivots, and fakes while their teammates move into open positions. A good point guard can control the ball with one hand and protect it with the other.

The most effective point guards fly up and down the court using each hand to dribble. This makes it very difficult for defenders to guard them. Once a point guard has mastered basic dribbling, he or she can practice trickier moves—like dribbling behind their back or through their legs—to confuse defenders.

Good point guards have confidence in their ball-handling abilities. While dribbling, they keep their eyes on the game, not on the ball.

PASSING THE BALL

With the point guard's central role in a team's offense, it is also very important for the player in this position to be a great passer. After all, basketball is a team game, and five players working together can always be more successful than one individual, no matter how skilled. Point guards need to know how to time their passes just right, sometimes putting a little zip on the ball, while other times lobbing it to an open teammate.

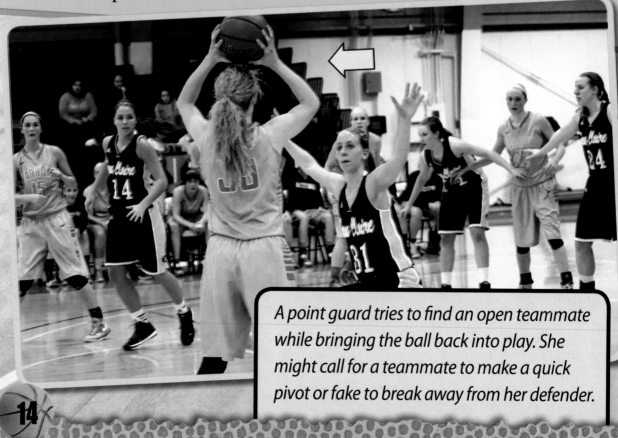

A point guard tries to find an open teammate while bringing the ball back into play. She might call for a teammate to make a quick pivot or fake to break away from her defender.

Point guard John Stockton holds the NBA record for most assists. He played his entire career with the Utah Jazz from 1984–2003. Stockton, who at 6'1" (1.8 m) was always one of the smallest players on the court, had an amazing 15,806 assists during his career.

Point guards are usually the players who get the most assists on any team, finding open teammates who can score. With their outstanding court vision and ability to read the game, truly great point guards often have several options when looking to pass. Then it is just a matter of choosing the teammate who is in the best position to score a basket.

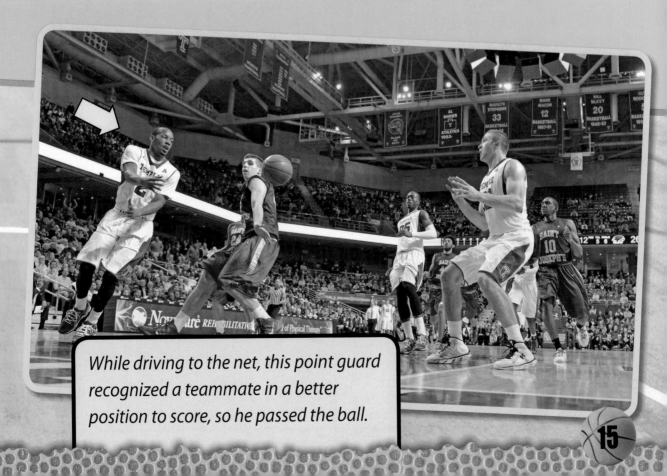

While driving to the net, this point guard recognized a teammate in a better position to score, so he passed the ball.

THE TYPES OF PASSES

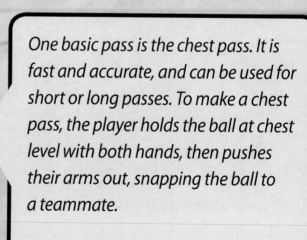

Good point guards use different kinds of passes to get the ball to open players and to throw off the defense. To make a bounce pass, the point guard bounces the ball off the court so that it will come up at their teammate's waist. It is effective for getting the ball around a defender and to a player who is in a better position to score.

One basic pass is the chest pass. It is fast and accurate, and can be used for short or long passes. To make a chest pass, the player holds the ball at chest level with both hands, then pushes their arms out, snapping the ball to a teammate.

For an overhead pass, the point guard holds the ball above their forehead, with their elbows bent at a right angle. The point guard then releases the ball, finishing with their arms fully extended. For a long baseball pass, the point guard sends the ball down the court with a motion that is similar to throwing a baseball or football. A more complicated pass is the behind-the-back pass. This move involves using one hand to wrap the ball behind a player's back before passing it to a teammate.

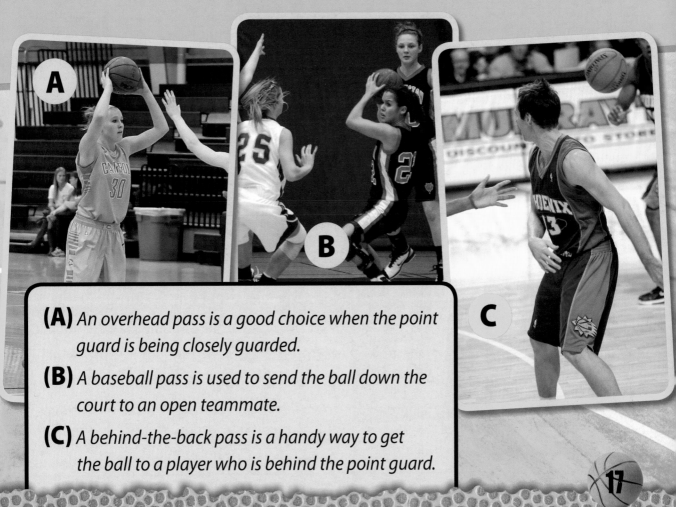

(A) *An overhead pass is a good choice when the point guard is being closely guarded.*

(B) *A baseball pass is used to send the ball down the court to an open teammate.*

(C) *A behind-the-back pass is a handy way to get the ball to a player who is behind the point guard.*

SHOOTING THE BALL

While a large part of a point guard's role on offense involves getting the ball to open teammates, he or she also needs to know how to make baskets and score. After all, if a defender knows that the point guard will never take a shot, it is much easier to defend against him or her. Learning and practicing proper shooting form from all over the court is important for any player in this position.

After taking a jump shot, it is important to follow through. At the end of the shot, the player's fingertips and elbow should be pointed toward the basket. This helps improve the ball's accuracy.

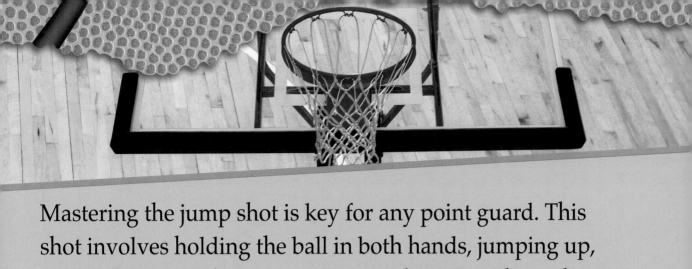

Mastering the jump shot is key for any point guard. This shot involves holding the ball in both hands, jumping up, and at the top of the jump, releasing the ball with one hand high above the head in an arc toward the basket.

Point guards must also master the **layup**, a running shot in which a player dribbles toward the basket, takes a legal two-step carry of the ball, and then "lays" it up softly, often off the backboard.

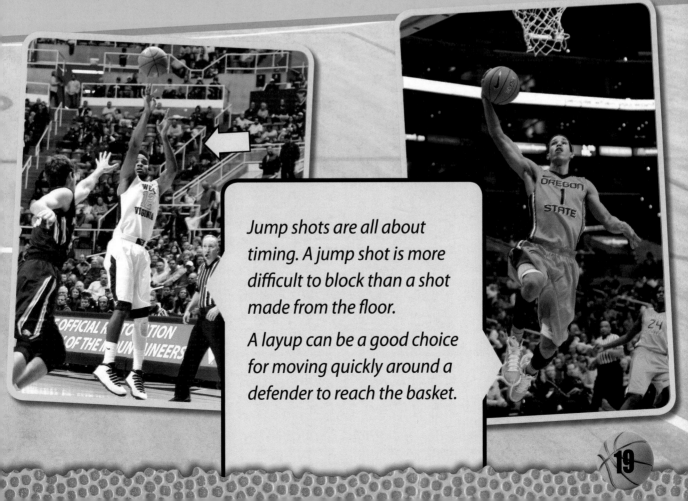

Jump shots are all about timing. A jump shot is more difficult to block than a shot made from the floor.

A layup can be a good choice for moving quickly around a defender to reach the basket.

MAKING THE SHOT

Many great point guards are masters of the **three-point shot**, a long-range basket scored from outside the three-point arc. In the NBA, the arc is 23 feet, 9 inches (7.24 m) away from the basket, except in the corners, where it is 22 feet (6.7 m) away. Point guards also need to be skilled at **free throws**, which are awarded by the referee when a player is fouled while taking a shot. Free throws are uncontested shots taken from behind a line that is 15 feet (4.6 m) from the basket. Each free throw is worth one point.

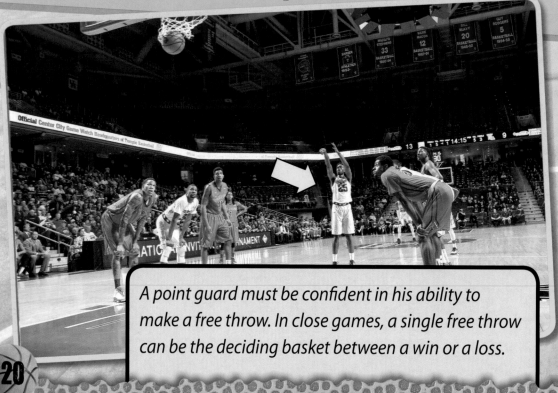

A point guard must be confident in his ability to make a free throw. In close games, a single free throw can be the deciding basket between a win or a loss.

The record for most points scored in a single game in the history of the WNBA is held by Tulsa Shock point guard Riquna Williams. In a game against the San Antonio Stars, she scored an incredible 51 points: 15 baskets from the floor (including an amazing 8 three-pointers) and 9 free throws.

Another important—and difficult—shot for a point guard to master is the "floater" or "runner." This shot is a cross between a jump shot and a layup. It is usually taken close to the basket, and "floated" over the defender to avoid being blocked. It takes a very soft touch to score with this tricky shot.

A floater shot is a good shot to master for times when a point guard is too close to the net to make a jump shot but too far out to go for a layup. With a high arc, a floater shot is hard for a defender to block.

PLAY OPTIONS

The fast break is one of the most exciting plays in basketball, and the point guard is almost always in the thick of the action. After winning a rebound, the team races up the court in an offensive attack before the defense can get set. With their excellent passing and dribbling skills, point guards usually lead the fast break and keep the action moving.

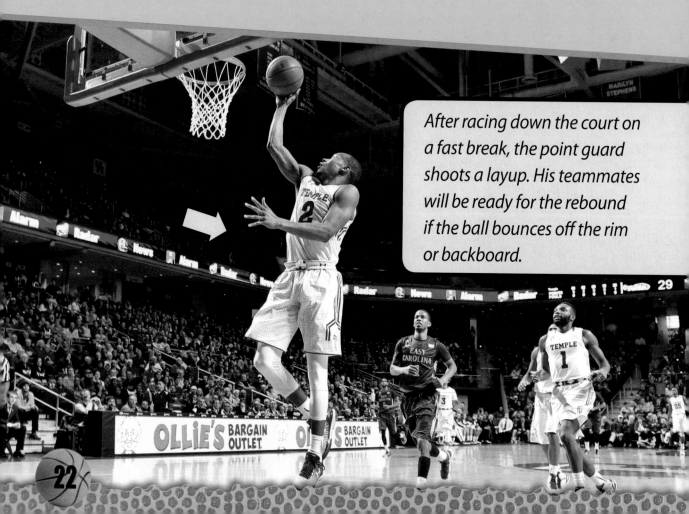

After racing down the court on a fast break, the point guard shoots a layup. His teammates will be ready for the rebound if the ball bounces off the rim or backboard.

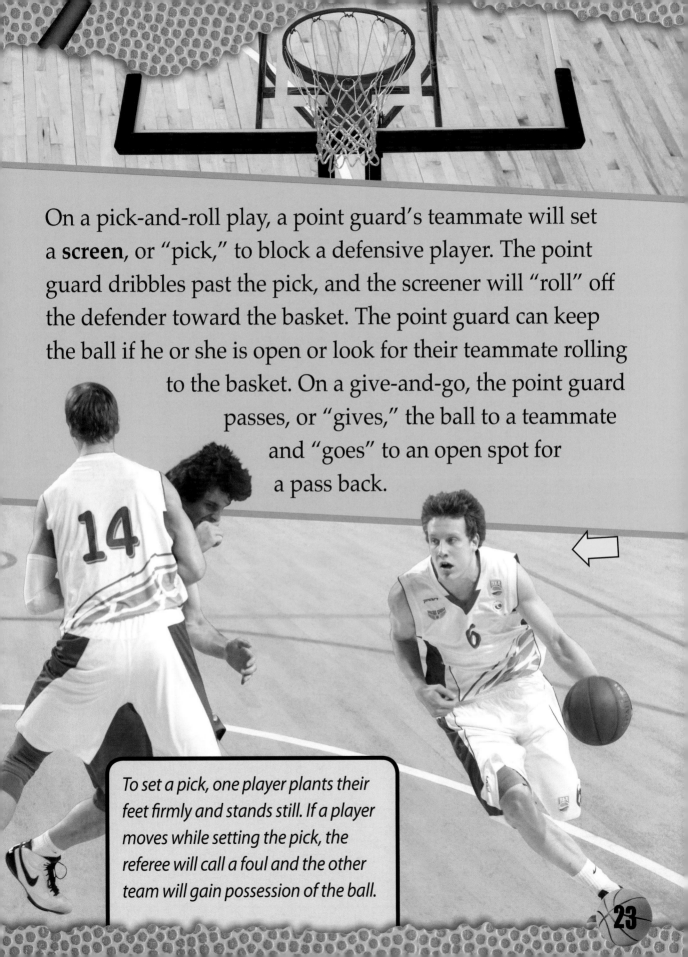

On a pick-and-roll play, a point guard's teammate will set a **screen**, or "pick," to block a defensive player. The point guard dribbles past the pick, and the screener will "roll" off the defender toward the basket. The point guard can keep the ball if he or she is open or look for their teammate rolling to the basket. On a give-and-go, the point guard passes, or "gives," the ball to a teammate and "goes" to an open spot for a pass back.

To set a pick, one player plants their feet firmly and stands still. If a player moves while setting the pick, the referee will call a foul and the other team will gain possession of the ball.

THE ROLE OF A COACH

All of the skills a point guard needs must be learned through hours of practice. Because of this player's important role on a team, the point guard should lead the squad in practice with an intense work ethic and discipline. Point guards often work harder than any other player on the team to improve their game. In games, point guards often become a "coach on the floor" as they lead their teammates on offense and defense.

Good communication between the point guard and coach is crucial. Before games and practices, they often discuss offensive and defensive tactics to have an effective game strategy ready to go.

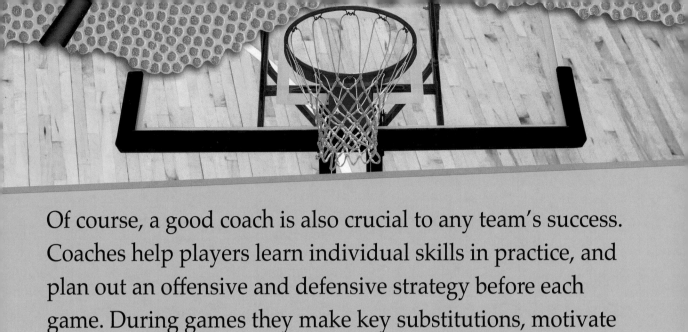

Of course, a good coach is also crucial to any team's success. Coaches help players learn individual skills in practice, and plan out an offensive and defensive strategy before each game. During games they make key substitutions, motivate players, and teach important lessons about respect for opponents and fans. It is safe to say that behind any great point guard or team, there is also a great coach!

A good coach recognizes each player's strengths, and works with them to improve weaknesses in their game. A coach stresses the importance of teamwork and good sportsmanship both on and off the court.

THE BEST POINT GUARDS

There have been hundreds of great point guards, and basketball fans love to debate about who the best all-time players in this position have been. Bob Cousy introduced a new blend of ball-handling and passing skills and revolutionized the position playing for the Boston Celtics from 1950–1963. Other early greats were Oscar Robertson and Walt Frazier.

Russell Westbrook (left) of the Oklahoma City Thunder is a four-time NBA All-Star and was the NBA scoring champion in 2015.

Chris Paul (right) of the Los Angeles Clippers has led the NBA in assists four times and steals six times.

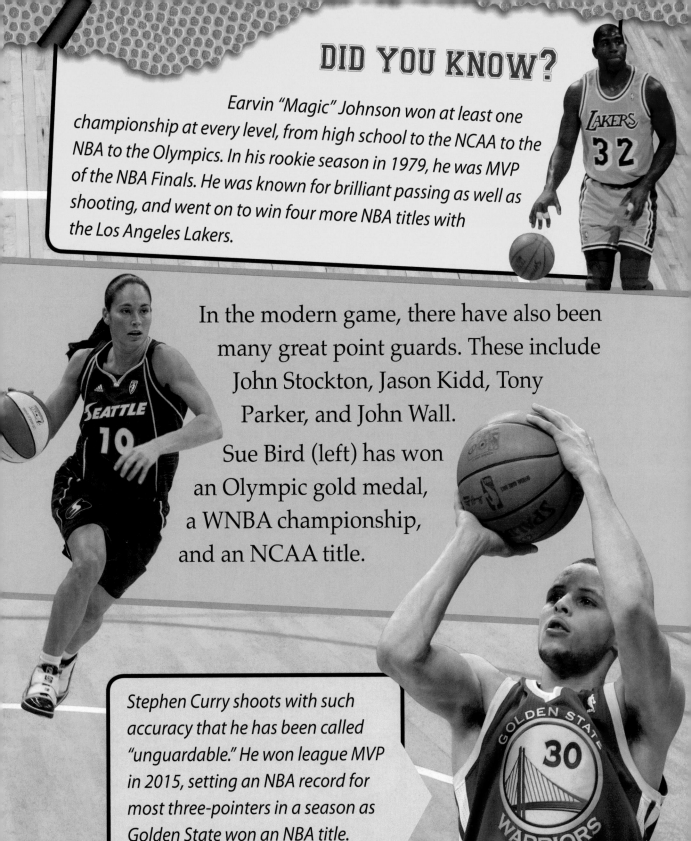

DID YOU KNOW?

Earvin "Magic" Johnson won at least one championship at every level, from high school to the NCAA to the NBA to the Olympics. In his rookie season in 1979, he was MVP of the NBA Finals. He was known for brilliant passing as well as shooting, and went on to win four more NBA titles with the Los Angeles Lakers.

In the modern game, there have also been many great point guards. These include John Stockton, Jason Kidd, Tony Parker, and John Wall.

Sue Bird (left) has won an Olympic gold medal, a WNBA championship, and an NCAA title.

Stephen Curry shoots with such accuracy that he has been called "unguardable." He won league MVP in 2015, setting an NBA record for most three-pointers in a season as Golden State won an NBA title. Curry broke his own record in 2016!

BE A GOOD SPORT

Good sportsmanship is very important to the game of basketball. Players, coaches, fans, referees, and parents all must remember to respect one another. Everyone likes to win, and in the heat of a game, it is easy to lose your cool. But trying to win should never be more important than acting in a positive way whether on the court, on the bench, or in the stands.

Players on the bench should cheer on and support their teammates and also pay attention to the action on the court.

As team leaders, point guards set an example for their teammates by being good sports. As "floor generals" in practice and in games, point guards are able to make sure every player gets involved in the action. They can lead by example with hard work and leadership so that everyone has fun, works hard, and plays with the respect the game deserves.

A good point guard leads their team both on and off the court, offers encouraging advice, and understands that there is no "I" in team.

GLOSSARY

assists Passes by one teammate that help others to score.

court vision In basketball, the ability to see plays develop and to notice the position of teammates and opponents.

defense When a team tries to stop their opponents from scoring.

dribble To move the ball up the court by bouncing it with one hand.

fakes In sports, pretend moves made to throw off an opponent.

foul Committing an infraction of the rules of basketball, as determined by the referee in an official game.

free throws Uncontested shots taken from the free-throw line that have been awarded after a foul.

key The area of a basketball court that is closest to the basket and marked off by a rectangle with a jump-ball circle at its top.

layup A shot taken by a player who dribbles, takes two quick steps while carrying the ball, and then shoots.

offense When a team has possession of the ball and is trying to score.

passing Throwing the ball through the air to a teammate.

rebound To catch the ball after it bounces off the rim or backboard.

referee The official who enforces the on-court rules of a basketball game.

screen An offensive move in which one player blocks a defender so another teammate can move past.

scrimmage To play an unofficial game.

steal To take the ball from another player.

three-point shot A long-range shot worth three points, taken from behind an arc on the court.

wing In basketball, one of the two sides of the court.

FOR MORE INFORMATION

FURTHER READING

Boone, Mary. *Sue Bird*. Mitchell Lane, 2012.

Doeden, Matt. *Basketball Legends in the Making*. Mankato, MN: Capstone, 2014.

Graves, Will. *The Best NBA Guards of All Time*. Edina, MN: ABDO, 2014.

Kaplan, Bobby. *Bball Basics for Kids*. Bloomington, IN: iUniverse, 2012.

WEBSITES

Due to the changing nature of Internet links, PowerKids Press has developed an online list of websites related to the subject of this book. This site is updated regularly. Please use this link to access the list:

www.powerkidslinks.com/bs/pguard

INDEX